# The 1880 United States Federal Census

*Explanations and Views*
*of the*
*Varied Eleven Forms*

**D. M. Kalten**

Copyright

The 1880 United States Federal Census
Explanations and Views of the Varied Eleven Forms

# Introduction

The U. S. government census records are questionnaires. Each census asks for names and facts for a variety of personal information. Questions can vary from one census to another, as you probably know.

The Federal United States Census for the year of 1880 has more to it than just the page you will find easily. There are other forms beyond the main form and few people realize that more information is available for their ancestors. Unfortunately many of the pay and free on-line sites show you only the main form and they do not hint that more information survives. Most people do not know that more information exists so they are happy with what they found and move on, missing a lot.

This book explains the different 1880 Federal United States Census forms and gives you information about each. You will see the instructions given to the enumerators and the questions asked of each household for each different form. You will also see a sample of each form.

If you have already done research for family members within the 1880 census, after reading this book, you will want to find what you have missed. If you are planning on doing research for the year of 1880, be sure to read this book first.

# Table of Contents

NOTES: _____

_____

_____

_____

_____

_____

_____

_____

x

# Chapter One. Explaining the Forms

The 1880 Federal Census was the tenth Federal United States Census, the first being done in 1790. The census began on the first day of June 1880 and was to be completed within thirty days. For areas with populations over 10,000 it was to be completed within two weeks. All information entered was to be as things were on or prior to the date of June 1, 1880. If something changed on June 2, it was not to be included.

Arrangement of the Census in microfilms is by the Enumeration District, often called the ED. This would be the area that one census taker could cover for the census.

When this census was completed, it showed that there were 50,189,209 residents in the country. The previous census of 1870 showed 39,818,449 residents.

...

Counting the main Federal census form, there were ten varied census forms for 1880. Another form to look at is the Mortality Schedule making the total forms eleven.

There were seven various supplemental forms connected to the main 1880 Federal census that many people are not aware of. These census forms fall under different classes and contained detailed information. Added forms were for the Insane, the Idiots, Deaf-Mutes, the Blind, Homeless Children, Prisoners and Paupers, and Indigent people. These are commonly known as the Social Statistic Schedules.

There were also the Agriculture, Manufacturing, and then the Mortality Schedules.

Schedules in the 1880 census were also known as the 'Decennial Census', those schedules being Agriculture, Manufacturing, Mortality, Population, and Social Statistics.

...

Each of the schedules was given a schedule name described as following.

(1) The MAIN Census, Schedule 1.

(2) INSANE:
1880 Supplemental Schedule 2, for the Defective, Dependent, and Delinquent Classes - INSANE.

(3) IDIOTS:
1880 Supplemental Schedule 3, for the Defective, Dependent, and Delinquent Classes – IDIOTS.

(4) DEAF-MUTES:
1880 Supplement Schedule 4, for the Defective, Dependent, and Delinquent Classes – DEAF-MUTES.

(5) BLIND:
1880 Supplement Schedule 5, for the Defective, Dependent, and Delinquent Classes – BLIND.

(6) HOMELESS CHILDREN:
1880 Supplement Schedule 6, for the Defective, Dependent, and Delinquent Classes – HOMELESS CHILDREN.

(7) PRISONERS:

1880 Supplement Schedule 7, for the Defective, Dependent, and Delinquent Classes – INHABITANTS IN PRISON.

(8) PAUPER and INDIGENT:

1880 Supplement Schedule 7 [7A], for the Defective, Dependent, and Delinquent Classes – PAUPER AND INDIGENT.

The above supplemental forms have been referred to as the DDD Census, meaning Defective, Dependent and Delinquent.

(9) AGRICULTURAL CENSUS. If your family member is listed as a farmer on the main census schedule, you do want to check this for further information concerning the person.

(10) MANUFACTURING. If your family member is shown owning a business connected to manufacturing, you do want to check this for further information concerning the person.

(11) MORTALITY. If you had a family member who died during the previous year, you do want to see this form.

...

4

# Chapter Two. Enumerators and Duties

## ENUMERATORS

Each enumerator was "to visit personally each dwelling house in his sub-division, and each family therein, and each individual living out of a family in any place of abode, and by inquiry made of the head of such family, or of the member there of deemed most credible and worthy of trust, or of such individual living out of a family, to obtain each and every item of information and all the particulars." In case no one was available at a family's usual place of abode, the enumerator was directed by the law "to obtain the required information, as nearly as may be practicable, from the family or families, or person or persons, living nearest to such place of abode."

...

## DUTIES OF ENUMERATORS

"It is by law made the duty of each enumerator, after being duly qualified as above, to visit personally each dwelling in his subdivision, and each family therein, and each individual living out of a family in any place of abode, and by inquiry made to the head of such family, or of the member hereof deemed most credible and worthy of trust, or of such individual living out of a family, to obtain each and every item of information and all the particulars required by the act of March 3, 1879, as amended by act of April 20, 1880.

"By individuals living out of families is meant all persons occupying lofts in public buildings, above stores, warehouses, factories, and stables, having no other usual place of abode; persons living solitary in cabins, huts, or tents; persons sleeping on river boats, canal boats, barges, etc., having no other usual place of abode, and persons in police stations having no homes. Of the classes just mentioned, the most important, numerically, is the first, viz.: those persons, chiefly in cities, who occupy rooms in public buildings, or above stores, warehouses, factories and stables. In order to reach such persons, the enumerator will need not only to keep his eyes open to all indications of such casual residence in his enumeration district, but to make inquiry both of the parties occupying the business portion of such buildings and also of the police. A letter will be addressed from this office to the mayor of every large city of the United States, requesting the cooperation of the police, so far as it may be necessary to prevent the omission of the classes of persons herein indicated.

"It is further provided by law that in case no person shall be found at the usual place of abode of such family, or individual living out of a family, competent to answer the inquiries made in compliance with the requirements of the act, then it shall be lawful for the enumerator to obtain the required information, as nearly as may be practicable, from the family or families, or persons or persons, living nearest to such place of abode.

"It is the prime object of the enumeration to obtain the name, and the requisite particulars as to personal description, of every person in the United States, of whatever age, sex, color, race, or condition, with this single exception, viz.: that "Indians not taxed" shall be omitted from the enumeration."

# INDIANS

Native American Indians that are not taxed are not in the regular population schedules but some may appear in special Indian schedules.

"By the phrase "Indians not taxed" is meant Indians living on reservations under the care of Government agents, or roaming individually, or in bands, over settled tracts of country.

"Indians, not in tribal relations, whether full-bloods or half-breeds, who are found mingled with the white population, residing in white families, engaged as servants or laborers, or living in huts or wigwams on the outskirts of towns or settlements are to be regarded as a part of the ordinary population of the country for the constitutional purpose of the apportionment of Representatives among the States, and are to be embraced in the enumeration."

...

# Chapter Three. Schedule 1

Schedule 1

The main 1880 Federal Census Schedule, Schedule 1.
Census office Form 7-296.

## Enumerator Instructions concerning 'Dwelling Houses':

"In column No. 1 of this schedule is to be entered the number of the dwelling house in the order of visitation. A dwelling house, for the purpose of the census, means any building or place of abode, of whatever character, material or structure, in which any person is at the time living, whether in a room above a warehouse or factory, a loft above a stable or a wigwam on the outskirts of a settlement, equally with a dwelling house in the usual, ordinary sense of that term. Wholly uninhabited dwellings are not to be taken notice of."

...

## Enumerator Instructions concerning 'Families':

"In the column numbered 2 is to be entered the number, in the order of visitation, of each family residing in the district. The word family, for the purposes of the census, includes persons living alone, as previously described, equally with families in the ordinary sense of that term, and also all larger aggregations of people having only the tie of a common roof and table. A hotel, with all its inmates, constitutes but one family within the meaning of this term. A hospital, a prison, an asylum is equally a family for the purposes of the census. On the other hand, the solitary inmate of a cabin, a loft, or a room finished off above a store constitutes a family in the meaning of the census act. In the case, however, of tenement houses and of the so-called "fiats" of the great cities, as many families are to be recorded as there are separate tables."

...

## Enumerator Instructions concerning 'Names':

"In entering names in column 3, the name of the father, mother, or other ostensible head of the family (in the case of hotels, jails, etc., the landlord, jailer, etc.) is to be entered first of the family. The family name is to be written first in the column, and the full first or characteristic Christian or "given" name of each member of the family in order thereafter. It is desirable that the children of the family proper should follow in the order of their ages, as will naturally be the case. So long as the family name remains the same for the several members, it need not be repeated, provided a distinct horizontal line or dash be drawn in the place it would occupy, thus:

Smith, John.

____, Elizabeth.

____, J. Henry."

...

## Enumerator Instructions concerning 'Personal Description':

"The columns 4, 5, and 6, which relate to age, sex, and color, must in every case be filled. No return will be accepted where these spaces are left blank.

...

"Ages.-The exact age in figures will be inserted in column 6 whenever the same can be obtained; otherwise, the nearest approximation thereto. Children who, on the 1st day of June, 1880, were less than a year old, will have their age stated by the fractional part of the year, as (one month), 1/12; (three months), 3/12; (nine months), 9/12, etc. In all other cases months will be omitted.

...

"Color.-It must not be assumed that, where nothing is written in this column, "white" is to be understood. The column is always to be filled. Be particularly careful in reporting the class mulatto. The word is here generic, and includes quadroons, octoroons, and all persons having any perceptible trace of African blood. Important scientific results depend upon the correct determination of this class in schedules 1 and 5."

...

## Enumerator Instructions concerning 'Occupation':

"In the column numbered 13 is to be reported the occupation of each person 10 years of age and upward.

"Occupation.- The inquiry "profession, occupation, or trade," is one of the most important questions of the schedule. Make a study of it. Take especial pains to avoid unmeaning terms, or such as are too general to convey a definite idea of the occupation. Call no man a "factory hand," or a "mill operative." State the kind of a mill or factory. The better form of expression would be, "Works in a cotton mill," "Works in paper mill," etc. Do not call a man a "shoemaker," "bootmaker," unless he makes the entire boot or shoe in a small shop. If he works in (or for) a boot or shoe factory, say so.

"Do not apply the word "jeweler" to those who make watches, watch chains, or jewelry in large manufacturing establishments.

"Call no man a "commissioner," a "collector," an "agent," an "artist," an "overseer," a "professor," a "treasurer," a "contractor," or a "speculator," without further explanation.

"When boys are entered as apprentices, state the trade they are apprenticed to, as "apprenticed to carpenter," "apothecary's apprentice." Students or scholars should be reported under those names.

"When a lawyer, a merchant, a manufacturer, has retired from practice or business, say "retired lawyer," "retired merchant," etc. Distinguish between fire and life insurance agents. When clerks are returned, describe them as "clerk in store," "clerk in woolen mill," "R.R. clerk," "bank clerk," etc.

"Describe no man as a "mechanic," if it is possible to describe him more accurately.

"Distinguish between stone masons and brick masons.

"Do not call a bonnet maker a bonnet manufacturer, a lace maker a lace manufacturer, a chocolate maker a chocolate manufacturer. Reserve the term "manufacturer" for proprietors of establishments; always give the branch of manufacture, as cotton manufacturer, woolen manufacturer, etc.

"Whenever merchants or traders can be reported under a single word expressive of their special line, as "grocer," it should be done. Otherwise say dry goods merchant, coal dealer, etc.

"Use the word "huckster" in all cases where it applies.

"Be very particular to distinguish between farmers and farm laborers. In agricultural regions this should be one of the points to which the enumerator should especially direct his attention.

"Confine the use of the words "glover," "hatter," and "furrier," to those who actual make, or make up, in their own establishments, all, or a part, of the gloves and hats or furs which they sell. Those who only sell these articles should be characterized as "glove dealer," "hat and cap dealer," "fur dealer."

"Judges (state whether Federal or state, whether probate, police, or otherwise) may be assumed to be lawyers, and that addition, therefore, need not be given; but all other officials should have their profession designated, if they have any, as "retired" merchant, governor of Massachusetts," "paper manufacturer, representative in legislature." If anything is to be omitted, leave out the office and put in the occupation.

"The organization of domestic service has not proceeded so far in this country as to render it worth while to make distinctions in the character of work. Report all as "domestic servants".

"Cooks, waiters, etc., in hotels and restaurants will be reported separately from domestic servants, as "cook in hotel", etc.

"The term "housekeeper" will be reserved for such persons as receive distinct wages or salary for the service. Women keeping house for their own families or for themselves, without any other gainful occupation, will be entered as "keeping house." Grown daughters assisting them will be reported without occupation.

"You are under no obligation to give any man's occupation just as he expresses it. If he can not tell intelligibly what it is, find out what he does and characterize his profession accordingly.

"The inquiry as to occupation will not be asked in respect to infants or children too young to take any part in production. Neither will the doing of domestic errands or family chores out of school be considered an occupation. "At home" or "attending school" will be the best entry in a majority of cases. But if a boy or girl, whatever the age, or earning money regularly by labor, contributing to the family support, or appreciably assisting in mechanical or agricultural industry, the occupation should be stated."

...

## Enumerator Instructions concerning 'Place of Birth':

"In column numbered 24 is to be reported the "Place of birth" of every person named upon the schedule. If born within the United States the State or Territory will be named, whether it be the State or Territory in which the person is at present residing or not. If of foreign birth, the country will be named as specifically as possible. Instead of writing "Great Britain" as the place of birth, give the particular country, as England, Scotland, Wales. Instead of "Germany" specify the State, as Prussia, Baden, Bavaria, Wurtemberg, Hesse-Darmstadt, etc."

…

## Enumerator Instructions concerning 'Civil Divisions':

"In filling schedule 1 the enumerator should begin each township (if there be more than one in a district), borough, etc., with a new page. The population of villages within townships should be carefully distinguished on the schedules. The population of such a village should, in all cases, begin with a new page; and when the inhabitants of a village have all been entered the remainder of the page should be left blank, except with the remark "Here ends the village of _____.

"So far as possible the population of small unincorporated villages and hamlets should be separately reported, as in the cases of incorporated villages and boroughs.

"Wherever an institution is to be enumerated, as a hospital, an asylum, an alms-house, a jail, or a penitentiary, the enumerator will leave three lines blank, and enter the name of the institution (as "St. Mary's Hospital," "Protestant Orphan Asylum," "Insane Asylum," "City jail," etc.) above the names and the inmates. All persons having their "usual place of abode" in such institutions, whether officers, attendants, beneficiaries, or persons in confinement, should then be entered consecutively on the schedules, and at the close of the list another space of three lines should be left blank."

...

## Enumerator Instructions concerning 'Numbering Pages':

"Each enumerator will number the pages of his population schedules in exact order as filled, and when filled: the first page (A) of the first sheet must be numbered 1; the second page of that sheet (B) 2, the third page (C) 3, the fourth page (D) 4, the first page of the second sheet 5, the first page of the third sheet 9, and so on throughout his entire subdivision.

"The enumerator should never place one sheet with another, but fill always the four pages of one sheet (in the order of the letters A, B, C, D) before making any entries on the next sheet."

...

## Enumerator Instructions concerning 'Streets and Street Numbers in Cities':

"The first two columns (not numbered in series) on the population schedule require the entry, in cities, of the street and street number of each occupied dwelling house. The name of the street should be written lengthwise of the space."

...

## The instructions at the top of the Census were:

NOTE A – The Census Year begins June 1, 1880, and ends May 31, 1880.

NOTE B – All persons will be included in the Enumeration who were living on the 1$^{st}$ day of June, 1880. No others will. Children BORN SINCE June 1, 1880, will be OMITTTED. Members of Families who have DIED SINCE June 1, 1880, will be INCLUDED.

NOTE C – Questions Nos. 13, 14, 22, and 23 are not to be asked in respect to persons under 10 years of age.

...

## The areas that were to be filled out at the top of the form were:

Page No.

Supervisor's Dist. No.

Enumeration Dist. No.

Inhabitants in _____, in the County of _____, State of _____, enumerated by me on the ____ day of June, 1880.

[Enumerator Signature] _____ Enumerator.

## The questions asked were:

In Cities. Name of Street.

In Cities. House Number.

1. Dwelling houses numbered in the order of visitation.

2. Families numbered in the order of visitation.

18

3. The name of each Person whose place of abode, on 1ˢᵗ day of June, 1880, was in this family.
4. Personal Description. Color – White, W; Black, B; Mulatto, Mu; Chinese, C; Italian, I.
5. Personal Description. Sex – Male (M), Female (F).
6. Personal Description. Age at last birth-day. If under 1 year, give months in fractions, thus 3/12.
7. If born within the Census year, give the month.
8. Relationship of each person to the head of this family – whether wife, son, daughter, servant, boarder, or other.
9. Civil Condition. Single.
10. Civil Condition. Married.
11. Civil Condition. Widowed, /. Divorced, D. [However enumerators often wrote 'W' for widowed.]
12. Civil Condition. Married during Census year.
13. Occupation. Profession, Occupation or Trade of each person, male or female.
14. Occupation. Number of months, this person has been unemployed during the Census year.
No number. Names
15. Health. Is the person [on the day of the Enumerator's visit] sick or temporarily disabled, so as to be unable to attend to ordinary business or duties? If so, what is the sickness or disability?
16. Health. Blind.
17. Health. Deaf and Dumb.
18. Health. Idiotic.
19. Health. Insane.
20. Health. Maimed, Crippled, Bedridden, or otherwise disabled.
21. Education. Attended school within the Census year.
22. Education. Cannot read.

23. Education. Cannot write.

24. Nativity. Place of Birth of this person, naming State or Territory of United States, or the Country, if of foreign birth.

25. Nativity. Place of Birth of the FATHER of this person, naming the State or Territory of United States, or the Country, if of foreign birth.

26. Nativity. Place of Birth of the MOTHER of this person, naming the State or Territory of United States, or the Country, if of foreign birth.

...

Following is a view of the 1880 heading from an original main form, Schedule 1, from Hamilton County, Cincinnati, Ohio.

[7—296.]

A.

Page No. 1

Supervisor's Dist. No. 104

Enumeration Dist. No. 123

Note A.—The Census Year begins June 1, 1879, and ends May 31, 1880.

Note B.—All persons will be included in the Enumeration who were living on the 1st day of June, 1880. No others will. Children BORN SINCE June 1, 1880, will be OMITTED. Members of Families who have DIED SINCE June 1, 1880, will be INCLUDED.

Note C.—Questions Nos. 13, 14, 22 and 23 are not to be asked to persons under 10 years of age.

SCHEDULE 1.—Inhabitants in Cincinnati , in the County of Hamilton , State of Ohio , enumerated by me on the ___ day of June, 1880.

Cattell H Phebe Enumerator.

# Chapter Four. Supplemental Schedule 2

SCHEDULE 2 – INSANE (Supplemental #1)

1880 Supplemental, Schedule 2, for the Defective, Dependent, and Delinquent Classes.

The INSANE Schedule 2 is shown in two parts at the end of this chapter. The upper instructions stated:

"The object of this Supplemental Schedule is to furnish material not only for a complete enumeration of the insane, but for an account of t heir condition. It is important that every inquiry respecting each case be answered as fully as possible. Enumerators will, therefore, after making the proper entries upon the population schedule (No. 1), transfer the name (with Schedule page and number) of every insane person found, from Schedule No. 1 to this Special Schedule, and proceed to ask the additional questions indicated in the headings of several columns.

Enumerators may obtain valuable hints as to the number of the insane, and their residence, from physicians who practice medicine in their respective districts."

The lower part of the second page gave the following rules:

**NOTE A** – An insane person may be found either at his own home or away from it in some institution, such as a hospital, asylum, or poor-house. In the latter case, his residence when at home must be stated, in order that he may be accredited to the State or county to which he properly belongs, and that the county in which the institution is situated may not be charged with more that its due proportion of insane.

**NOTE B** – It is not necessary to make minute subdivisions, but to ascertain the number suffering from certain marked forms of insanity – mania, melancholia, paresis (general paralysis), dementia, epilepsy or dipsomania.

**NOTE C** – An insane person may have more than one attack of insanity. He may recover and afterward become again insane. It is important to know at what age the first attack occurred; how many distinct attacks the patient has had; and the duration of the present attack. If he has not had more than one attack, which still continues, insert the figure "1" in column 9. The duration of the present attack may be stated in years or months, this: "1 yr." or "3 mos."

**NOTE D** – The object of the inquiries in columns 11 and 12 is to ascertain approximately the proportion of the insane who cannot be trusted with their personal freedom. In column 11, if the patient is usually or often locked in a room or other apartment in the day time, say "yes" if not, say "no;" but if locked at night and not by day, say "night." In column 12, if usually or often mechanically restrained, state the mode of restraint, thus: strait-jacket, camisole, muff, strap, hand cuffs, ball and chain, crib-bed, etc. If, instead of mechanical restraint, the patient has a constant personal attendant, say "attendant."

**NOTE E** – In column 13 name all the hospitals or asylums for the insane (not jails or poor-houses) in which the patient has been for a longer or shorter time as inmate, and in column 14 state the entire number of months or years spent in such institutions (whether in one institution or more).

NOTE F – In making entries in columns 16, 17, and 18, an affirmative mark only will be used, thus /.

The questions asked:
1. Number taken from Schedule No. 1. Number of page.
2. Number taken from Schedule No. 1. Number of Line.
3. Name.
4. Residence when at home. – (See note A.) City or Town.
5. Residence when at home. (See note A.) County (if in same State), or State (if in some other State).
6. If now an inmate of an institution, is this person a pay patient?
7. Form of Disease. (See note B.)
8. History of attack. (See note C.) Duration of present attack, (not including previous attacks.)
9. History of attack. (See note C.) Total number of attacks, (including the present on.)
10. History of attack. (See note C.) Age at which first attack occurred.
11. Restraint and Seclusion. – (See note D.) Does this person require to be usually or often kept in a cell or other apartment under lock and key, either by day or at night?
12. Restraint and Seclusion. – (See note D.) Does this person require to be usually or often restrained by any mechanical appliance, such as a strap, strait-jacket, etc.? and if yes, state the character of the appliance used.
13. Hospital or Asylum. – (See note E.) Has this person ever been an inmate of any hospital or asylum for the insane? If yes, name the said hospital or asylum.
14. Hospital or Asylum. – (See note E.) What has been the total length of time spent by him (or her) during life in such asylums?

15. Hospital or Asylum. – (See note E.) Date of discharge (year only).

16. See Note F. Is this person also an epileptic?

17. See Note F. Is this person suicidal?

18. See Note F. Is this person homicidal?

Supplemental Schedule 2 follows in two parts.

# 1880 Supplemental Schedule 2, for the Defective, Dependent, and Delinquent Classes

## INSANE inhabitants in _____, in the County of _____, State of _____.

Enumerated by me June, 1880. _____, Enumerator.

Supervisor's Dist No. _____
Enumeration Dist No. _____

The object of this Supplemental Schedule is to furnish material not only for a complete enumeration of the insane, but for an account of their condition. It is important that every inquiry respecting each case be answered as fully as possible. Enumerators will, therefore, *after making the proper entries upon the Population Schedule (No. 1)*, transfer the name (with Schedule page and number) of every insane person found, from Schedule No. 1 to this Special Schedule, and proceed to ask the *additional questions* indicated in the headings of several columns. Enumerators may obtain valuable hints as to the number of the insane, and their residence, from physicians who practice medicine in their respective districts.

| Number taken from Schedule No. 1 | | Name | Residence when at home. — (See note A.) | | If now an inmate of an institution, is this person a pay-patient? | Form of Disease. (See note B.) |
| Number of page | Number of Line | | City or Town | County (if in same State), or State (if in some other State) | | |
| 1 | 2 | 3 | 4 | 5 | 6 | 7 |
| 1 | | | | | | |
| 2 | | | | | | |
| 3 | | | | | | |
| 4 | | | | | | |
| 5 | | | | | | |

| | History of attack (See note C) | | | Restraint and Seclusion – (See note D) | | Hospital or Asylum. – (See note E.) | | | See Note F. | | |
|---|---|---|---|---|---|---|---|---|---|---|---|
| | Duration of present attack, (not including previous attacks) | Total number of attacks, (including the present one) | Age at which first attack occurred | Does this person require to be usually or often kept in a cell or other apartment under lock and key, either by day or at night? | Does this person require to be usually or often restrained by any mechanical appliance, such as a strap, strait-jacket, etc? and if yes, state the character of the appliance used | Has this person ever been an inmate of any hospital or asylum for the insane? If yes, name the said hospital or asylum | What has been the total length of time spent by him (or her) during life in such asylums? | Date of discharge (year only) | Is this person also an epileptic? | Is this person suicidal? | Is this person homicidal? |
| | 8 | 9 | 10 | 11 | 12 | 13 | 14 | 15 | 16 | 17 | 18 |
| 1 | | | | | | | | | | | |
| 2 | | | | | | | | | | | |
| 3 | | | | | | | | | | | |
| 4 | | | | | | | | | | | |
| 5 | | | | | | | | | | | |

NOTE A – An insane person may be found either at his own home or away from it in some institution, such as a hospital, asylum, or poor-house. In the latter case, his residence when at home must be stated, in order that he may be accredited to the State or county to which he properly belongs, and that the county in which the institution is situated may not be charged with more than its due proportion of insane.

NOTE B – It is not necessary to make minute subdivisions, but to ascertain the number suffering from certain marked forms of insanity—mania, melancholia, paresis (general paralysis) dementia, epilepsy or dipsomania.

NOTE C – An insane person may have more than one attack of insanity: he may recover and afterward become again insane. It is important to know at what age the first attack occurred, how many distinct attacks the patient has had, and the duration of the present attack. *If he has not had more than one attack which still continues, insert the figure "1" in column 9.* The duration of the present attack may be stated in years or months, thus: "1 yr" or "3 mos."

NOTE D – The object of the inquiries in columns 11 and 12 is to ascertain approximately the proportion of the insane who cannot be trusted with their personal freedom. In column 11, if the patient is usually or often locked in a room or other apartment in the day time, say "yes;" if not, say "no;" "but if locked at night and not by day, say "night." In column 12, if usually or often mechanically restrained, state the mode of restraint, thus: strait-jacket, camisole, muff, strap, band-cuff, ball and chain, crib-bed, etc. If instead of mechanical restraint, the patient has a constant personal attendant, say "attendant."

NOTE E – In column 13 name all the hospitals or asylums for the insane (not jails or poor-houses) in which the patient has been for a longer or shorter time an inmate, and in column 14 state the entire number of months or years spent in such institutions (whether in one institution or more).

NOTE F – In making entries in columns 16, 17, and 18, an affirmative mark only will be used, thus: /

# Chapter Five. Supplemental Schedule 3

SCHEDULE 3 – IDIOTS (Supplemental #2)

1880 Supplemental Schedule 3, for the Defective, Dependent, and Delinquent Classes.

The IDIOT Schedule upper instructions stated:
"The object of this Supplemental schedule is to furnish material not only for a complete enumeration of the idiots, but for an account of their condition. It is important that every inquiry respecting each case b answered as fully as possible. Enumerators will, therefore, after making the proper entries upon the population schedule (No. 1), transfer the name (with Schedule paper and number) of every idiot found, from Schedule No.1 to this Special Schedule, and proceed to ask the additional questions indicated in the headings of the several columns.

The word "idiot" has a special meaning which it is essential for every enumerator to know. An idiot is a person the development of whose development of whose mental facilities was arrested in infancy or childhood before coming to maturity. It is sometimes difficult to distinguish between the stupidity which results from Idiocy and that which is due to the loss or deterioration of mental power in consequence of insanity. The latter is not true idiocy, but dementia or imbecility. The enumeration desired for the Census is of true idiots only. Demented persons should be classed with the insane.

Enumerators may obtain valuable hints as to the number of idiots, and their residences, from physicians who practice medicine in their respective districts."

The lower part of the second part gave the following rules:

**NOTE A** – An idiot may be found either at his own home or away from it in some institution, such as a training school, asylum, or poor-house. In the latter case, his residence when at home must be stated, in order that he may be accredited to the State or county which he properly belongs, and that the county to which the institution is situated may not be charged with more than its due proportion of idiots.

**NOTE B** – If self-supporting, say "yes," if partly self-supporting, say "partly," if not, say "no." Indicate all inmates of institutions who are maintained or treated at their personal expense (not at the expense of any town, county, or State, nor of the institution) by the word "Pay."

**NOTE C** – If an idiot from birth, say "B," if idiocy occurred after birth, state the age at which it occurred. Special pains should be taken to indicate all idiots from birth.

**NOTE D** – The causes of idiocy are such as the following: scarlet fever, measles, meningitis, etc, blow on head, fall, etc, fright, etc.

**NOTE E** – In making entries in columns 13, 14, 15, 16, 17, and 18, an affirmative mark only will be used, thus /.

The questions asked:

1. Number taken from Schedule No. 1 – Number of page.
2. Number taken from Schedule No. 1 – Number of line.
3. Name.
4. Residence when at home. (See Note A.) City or Town.
5. Residence when at home. County (if in same State), or State (if in some other State).
6. Is this person self-supporting, or partly so? (See Note B.)

7. Age at which idiocy occurred. (See Note C.)

8. Supposed Cause of idiocy (if acquired). (See Note D.)

9. Size of head. (Large, small, or natural.)

10. Has this person ever been an inmate of a training school for idiots? If yes, name the said training school.

11. What has been the total length of time spent by him (or her) during life in any such training school or training schools?

12. Date of discharge. (Year only.)

13. Is this person also insane> /. See Note E.)

14. Is he (or she) also blind? /. (See Note E.)

15. Is he (or she) also deaf? /. (See Note E.)

16. Is he (or she also an epileptic? /. (See Note E.)

17. Is he (or she) paralyzed? And if yes, on which side? Right. /. (See Note E.)

18. Is he (or she) paralyzed? And if yes, on which side? Left. /. (See Note E.)

The IDIOT Schedule follows in two parts:

# 1880 Supplemental Schedule 3, for the Defective, Dependent, and Delinquent Classes

Inhabitants in _____, in the County of _____, State of _____

Supervisor's Dist. No. _____

Enumeration Dist No. _____

Enumerated by me June, 1880.

## IDIOTS.

The object of this Supplemental Schedule is to furnish material not only for a complete enumeration of the idiots, but for an account of their condition. It is important that every inquiry respecting each case be answered as fully as possible. Enumerators will therefore, *after making the proper entries upon the Population Schedule (No. 1)*, transfer the name (with Schedule paper and number) of every idiot found, from Schedule No. 1 to this Special Schedule, and proceed to ask the *additional questions* indicated in the headings of the several columns.

The word "idiot" has a special meaning which it is essential for every enumerator to know. An idiot is a person the development of whose mental faculties was arrested *in infancy or childhood before coming to maturity.* It is sometimes difficult to distinguish between the stupidity which results from idiocy and that which is due to the loss or deterioration of mental power in consequence of insanity. The latter is not true idiocy, but dementia or imbecility. The enumeration desired for the Census is of *true idiots only.* Demented persons should be classed with the insane.

Enumerators may obtain valuable hints as to the number of idiots, and their residences, from physicians who practice medicine in their respective districts.

| Number taken from Schedule No. 1. | | Name | Residence when at home. (See Note A.) | | Is this person self-supporting, or partly so? (See Note B.) | Age at which idiocy occurred. (See Note C.) | Supposed Cause of idiocy (if acquired). (See Note D.) | Size of head (Large, small, or natural.) |
|---|---|---|---|---|---|---|---|---|
| Number of page. | Number of line. | | City or Town. | County (if in same State), or State (if in some other State) | | | | |
| 1 | 2 | 3 | 4 | 5 | 6 | 7 | 8 | 9 |
| 1 | | | | | | | | |
| 2 | | | | | | | | |
| 3 | | | | | | | | |
| 4 | | | | | | | | |
| 5 | | | | | | | | |

| Training School | | | (See Note E) | | | | | |
|---|---|---|---|---|---|---|---|---|
| Has this person ever been an inmate of a training school for idiots? If yes, name the said training school | What has been the total length of time spent by him (or her) during life in any such training school or training school? | Date of discharge (Year only) | Is this person also insane? | Is he (or she) also blind? | Is he (or she) also deaf? | Is he (or she) also an epileptic? | Is he (or she) paralyzed? And if yes, on which side? Right / | Left / |
| 10 | 11 | 12 | 13 | 14 | 15 | 16 | 17 | 18 |
| | | | | | | | | |
| | | | | | | | | |
| | | | | | | | | |
| | | | | | | | | |
| | | | | | | | | |

NOTE A – An idiot may be found either at his own home or away from it in some institution, such as a training school, asylum, or poor-house. In the latter case, his residence when at home must be stated, in order that he may be accredited to the State or county to which he properly belongs, and that the county in which the institution is situated may not be charged with more than its due proportion of idiots.

NOTE B – If self-supporting, say "yes," if partly self-supporting, say "partly," if not, say "no." Indicate all inmates of institutions who are maintained or treated at their personal expense (not at the expense of any town, county, or State, nor of the institution) by the word "Pay."

NOTE C – If an idiot from birth, say "B," if idiocy occurred after birth, state the age at which it occurred. Special pains should be taken to indicate all idiots from birth.

NOTE D – The causes of idiocy are such as the following, scarlet fever, measles, meningitis, etc., blow on head fall, etc, fright, etc.

NOTE E – In making entries in columns 13, 14, 15, 16, 17, and 18, an affirmative mark only will be used, thus /

# Chapter Six. Supplemental Schedule 4

SCHEDULE 4 – DEAF-MUTES (Supplemental #3)

1880 Supplement Schedule 4, for the Defective, Dependent, and Delinquent Classes.

The DEAF-MUTES Schedule upper instructions stated:
'The object of this Supplemental Schedule is to furnish material not only for a complete numeration of deaf-mutes, but for an account of their condition. It is important that every inquiry respecting each case be answered as fully as possible. Enumerators will, therefore , after making the proper entries upon the Population Schedule (No 1), transfer the name (with Schedule page and number) of every deaf-mute found, from Schedule No. 1 to this Special Schedule, and proceed to ask the additional questions indicated in the headings of the several columns. Care must be taken not to enumerate persons who are deaf only (hard of hearing) or dub only (tongue-tied) as deaf-mutes. A deaf-mute is one who cannot speak, because he cannot hear sufficiently well to learn to speak.
Enumerators may obtain valuable hints as to the number of deaf-mutes, and their residence, from physicians who practice medicine in their respective districts, also from school-teachers. Great assistance may be derived from questions addressed to deaf-mutes themselves: Do you know any deaf-mutes in this neighborhood? The class feeling of the deaf and dumb, arising from their isolated state, is so great that they seek each other out for the sake of companionship and ordinarily know every deaf-mute for miles around.'

The lower part of the schedule gave the following rules:

**NOTE A** – A deaf-mute may be found either at his own home or away from it in some educational institution, asylum, or poor-house. In the latter case, his residence when at home must be stated, in order that he may be a credited to the State or county to which he properly belongs, and that the county in which the institution is situated may not be charged with more than its due proportion of deaf-mutes.

**NOTE B** – If self-supporting, say "yes," if partly self-supporting, say "partly," if not, say "no". Indicate all inmates of institutions who are maintained or treated at their personal expense (not at the expense of any town, county, or State, nor of the institution) by the word "Pay."

**NOTE C** – If a deaf-mute from birth, say "B," if idiocy occurred after birth, state the age at which deafness occurred. Special pains should be taken to indicate all deaf mutes from birth.

**NOTE D** – The word "semi-mute" has a technical meaning, and denotes a deaf-mute who lost his or her hearing after having acquired at least a partial knowledge of spoken language. Some semi-mutes retain the ability to speak imperfectly, others lose it entirely. If a deaf-mute has ever learned to speak, he is semi-mute; (unless he was artificially taught to peak in an institution for deaf-mutes.) By a semi-deaf person is meant one who cannot hear sufficiently well to comprehend what is said to him but who hears very loud sounds, such as thunder, etc.

**NOTE E** – In making entries in columns, 13, 15, and 16, an affirmative mark only will be used, thus /.

The questions asked:

1. Number taken from Schedule No. 1. Number of page.

2. Number taken from Schedule No. 1. Number of line.

3. Name.

4. Residence when at home. (See Note A.) City or Town.

5. Residence when at home. (See Note A.) County (if in same State), or State (if in some other State).

6. Is he (or she) self-supporting, or partly so? (See Note B.)

7. Age at which deafness, occurred. (See Note C.)

8. Supposed Cause of deafness, if known.

9. See Note D. Is this person semi-mute?

10. See Note D. Is he (or she) semi-deaf?

11. Institution life. Has this person ever been an inmate of an institution for deaf-mute? If yes, give the name of such institution.

12. Institution life. What has been the total length of time spent by him (or her) in any such institution?

13. Institution life. Date of his (or her) discharge. (Year only.)

14. See Note E. Is this person also insane?

15. See Note E. Is he (or she) also idiotic?

16. See Note E. Is he (or she) also blind?

The DEAF- MUTES Schedule follows in two parts:

# 1880 Supplemental Schedule 4, for the Defective, Dependent, and Delinquent Classes

Inhabitants in _____, in the County of _____, State of _____

Supervisor's Dist. No. _____

Enumeration Dist No. _____

Enumerated by me June, 1880.

## DEAF-MUTES.

The object of this Supplemental Schedule is to furnish material not only for a complete enumeration of deaf-mutes, but for an account of their condition. It is important that every inquiry respecting each case be answered as fully as possible. Enumerators will, therefore, *after making the proper entries upon the Population Schedule (No. 1),* transfer the name (with Schedule page and number) of every deaf-mute found from Schedule No. 1 to this Special Schedule, and proceed to ask the *additional questions* indicated in the headings of the several columns. Care must be taken not to enumerate persons who are deaf only (hard of hearing) or dumb only (tongue-tied) as deaf-mutes. A deaf-mute is one who cannot speak, because he cannot hear sufficiently well to learn to speak. Enumerators may obtain valuable hints as to the number of deaf-mutes, and their residence, from physicians who practice medicine in their respective districts, also from school-teachers. Great assistance may be derived from questions addressed to deaf-mutes themselves. Do you know any deaf-mutes in this neighborhood? The class feeling of the deaf and dumb, arising from their isolated state, is so great that they seek each other out for the sake of companionship and ordinarily know every deaf-mute for miles around.

| Number taken from Schedule No. 1 | | Name | Residence when at home. (See Note A.) | | Is he (or she) self-supporting, or partly so? (See Note B.) | Age at which deafness occurred (See Note C.) | Supposed Cause of deafness, if known. |
| Number of page | Number of line | | City or Town. | County (if in same State), or State (if in some other State) | | | |
| 1 | 2 | 3 | 4 | 5 | 6 | 7 | 8 |
| | | | | | | | |
| | | | | | | | |
| | | | | | | | |
| | | | | | | | |
| | | | | | | | |

| See Note D. | | Institution life. | | | See Note E. | | |
|---|---|---|---|---|---|---|---|
| 9 | 10 | 11 | 12 | 13 | 14 | 15 | 16 |
| Is this person semi-mute? | Is he (or she) semi-deaf? | Has this person ever been an inmate of an institution for deaf-mutes? If yes, give the name of such institution on | What has been the total length of time spent by him (or her) in any such institution? | Date of his (or her) discharge (Year only) | Is this person also insane? | Is he (or she) also idiotic? | Is he (or she) also blind? |
| | | | | | | | | 1 |
| | | | | | | | | 2 |
| | | | | | | | | 3 |
| | | | | | | | | 4 |
| | | | | | | | | 5 |

NOTE A – A deaf-mute may be found either at his own home or away from it in some educational institution, asylum, or poor-house. In the latter case, his residence when at home must be stated, in order that he may be accredited to the State or county to which he properly belongs, and that the county in which the institution is situated may not be charged with more than its due proportion of deaf-mutes.

NOTE B – If self-supporting, say "yes," if partly self-supporting, say "partly," if not, say "no." Indicate all inmates of institutions who are maintained or treated at their personal expense (not at the expense of any town, county, or State, nor of the institution) by the word "Pay."

NOTE C – If a deaf-mute from birth, say "B," if idiocy occurred after birth, state the age at which deafness occurred. Special pains should be taken to indicate all deaf-mutes from birth.

NOTE D – The word "semi-mute" has a technical meaning, and denotes a deaf-mute who lost his or her hearing after having acquired at least a partial knowledge of spoken language. Some semi-mutes retain the ability to speak imperfectly, others lose it entirely. If a deaf-mute has ever learned to speak, he is a semi-mute, (unless he was artificially taught to speak in an institution for deaf-mutes.) By a semi-deaf person is meant one who cannot hear sufficiently well to comprehend what is said to him but who hears very loud sounds, such as thunder, etc.

NOTE E – In making entries in columns 14, 15, and 16, an affirmative mark only will be used, thus /

# Chapter Seven. Supplemental Schedule 5

SCHEDULE 5 – BLIND (Supplemental #4)

1880 Supplement Schedule 5, for the Defective, Dependent, and Delinquent Classes – BLIND.

The BLIND Schedule upper instructions stated:
'The object of this Supplemental Schedule is to furnish material not only for a complete enumeration of the blind, but for an account of their condition. It is important that every inquiry respecting each case be answered as fully as possible. Enumerators will, therefore, after making the proper entries upon the Population Schedule (No. 1), transfer the name (with Schedule paper and number) of ever blind person found, from Schedule No. 1 to this Special Schedule, and proceed to ask the additional questions indicated in the headings of the several columns.

In this enumeration will be included not only the totally blind, but also the semi-blind. No person will be carried on this Schedule, however, who can see sufficiently well to read. For the distinction between the totally blind and the semi-blind see Note E; it is of the greatest importance to note this distinction with care, by making the proper entry in columns 10 or 11.'

The lower part of the second part gave the following rules:
**NOTE A** – A blind person may be found either at his own home or away from it in some educational institution, asylum, or poor-house. In the latter case, his residence when at home must be stated, in order that he may be accredited to the State or county to which he properly

belongs, and that the county in which the institution is situated may not be charged with more that its due proportion of the blind.

**NOTE B** – If self-supporting, say "yes," if partly self-supporting, say "partly," if not, say "no." Indicate all inmates of institutions who are maintained or treated at their personal expense (not at the expense of any town, county, or State, nor of the institution) by the word "Pay."

**NOTE C** – If blind from birth, say "B," if not, state the age at which blindness occurred. Special pains should be taken to indicate all the blind from birth.

**NOTE D** – Where practicable, get a statement from the attending physician.

**NOTE E** – The totally blind are unable to distinguish forms of colors; the partially blind can distinguish forms or colors, but cannot see to read, or at least not without such effort as to make reading practically impossible.

NOTE F – In making entries in columns 10, 11, 15, 16, and 17, an affirmative mark only will be used, thus /.

The questions asked:

1. Number taken from Schedule No. 1. Number of page.

2. Number taken from Schedule No. 1. Number of line.

3. Name.

4. Residence when at home. (See Note A.) City or Town.

5. Residence when at home. (See Note A.) County (if in same State), or State (if in some other State).

6. Is he (or she) self-supporting, or partly so? (See Note B.)

7. Age at which blindness occurred. (See Note C.)

8. Form of blindness. (See Note D.)

9. Supposed cause of blindness, if know.

10. See Note F. Is this person totally blind? (See Note E.)

11. See Note F. Is this person semi-blind? (See Note E.)

12. Institutional life. Has this person ever been an inmate of an institution for the blind? If yes, give the name of such institution.

13. Institutional life. What has been the total length of time spent by him (or her) in any such institution?

14. Institutional life.

15. (See Note F.) Is this person also Insane?

16. (See Note F.) Is he (or she) also idiotic?

17. (See Note F.) Is he (or she) also a deaf-mute?

The BLIND Schedule follows in two parts:

# 1880 Supplemental Schedule 5, for the Defective, Dependent, and Delinquent Classes

Inhabitants in _____, in the County of _____, State of _____

Supervisor's Dist. No. _____

Enumeration Dist. No. _____

Enumerated by me June, 1880.

## BLIND.

The object of this Supplemental Schedule is to furnish material not only for a complete enumeration of the blind, but for an account of their condition. It is important that every inquiry respecting each case be answered as fully as possible. Enumerators will, therefore, *after making the proper entries upon the Population Schedule (No. 1)*, transfer the name (with Schedule paper and number) of every blind person found, from Schedule No. 1 to this Special Schedule, and proceed to ask the *additional questions* indicated in the headings of the several columns.

In this enumeration will be included not only the totally blind, but also the semi-blind. No person will be carried on this Schedule, however, who can see sufficiently well to read. For the distinction between the totally blind and the semi-blind see Note E, it is of the greatest importance to note this distinction with care, by making the proper entry in columns 10 or 11.

| Number taken from Schedule No. 1 | | Name | Residence when at home. (See Note A.) | | Is he (or she) self-supporting, or partly so? (See Note B.) | Age at which blindness occurred. (See Note C.) | Form of blindness. (See Note D.) | Supposed cause of blindness, if know |
|---|---|---|---|---|---|---|---|---|
| Number of page. | Number of line. | | City or Town. | County (if in same State). or State (if in some other State). | | | | |
| 1 | 2 | 3 | 4 | 5 | 6 | 7 | 8 | 9 |
| 1 | | | | | | | | |
| 2 | | | | | | | | |
| 3 | | | | | | | | |
| 4 | | | | | | | | |
| 5 | | | | | | | | |

| See Note F. | | Institution life. | | | See Note F. | | |
|---|---|---|---|---|---|---|---|
| Is this person totally blind? (See Note E) | Is this person semi-blind? (See Note E) | Has this person ever been an inmate of an institution for the blind? If yeas, give the name of such institution | What has been the total length of time spent by him (or her) in any such institution? | Date of his (or her) discharge. (Year only) | Is this person also insane? | Is he (or she) also idiotic? | Is he (or she) also a deaf-mute? |
| 10 | 11 | 12 | 13 | 14 | 15 | 16 | 17 |
| | | | | | | | |
| | | | | | | | |
| | | | | | | | |
| | | | | | | | |
| | | | | | | | |

NOTE A – A blind person may be found either at his own home or away from it in some educational institution, asylum, or poor-house. In the latter case, his residence when at home must be stated, in order that he may be accredited to the State or county to which he properly belongs, and that the county in which the institution is situated may not be charged with more that its due proportion of the blind.

NOTE B – If self-supporting, say "yes;" if partly self-supporting, say "partly;" if not, say "no." Indicate all inmates of institutions who are maintained or treated at their personal expense (not at the expense of any town, county, or State, nor of the institution) by the word "Pay."

NOTE C – If a blind from birth, say "B," if not, state the age at which blindness occurred. Special pains should be taken to indicate all the blind from birth.

NOTE D – Where practicable, get a statement from attending physician.

NOTE E – The totally blind are unable to distinguish forms of colors; the partially-blind can distinguish forms or colors, but cannot see to read, or at least not without such effort as to make reading practically impossible.

NOTE F – In making entries in columns 10, 11, 15, 16, and 17, an affirmative mark only will be used, thus /

# Chapter Eight. Supplemental Schedule 6

SCHEDULE 6 – HOMELESS CHILDREN (Supplemental #5)

1880 Supplement Schedule 6, for the Defective, Dependent, and Delinquent Classes – HOMELESS CHILDREN.

The HOMELESS CHILDREN Schedule upper instructions stated:
The object of this Supplemental Schedule is to furnish material not only for a complete enumeration of children in institutions, but for an account of their condition. it is important that every inquiry respecting each case be answered as fully as possible. Enumerators will, therefore, after making the proper entries upon the Population Schedule (No. 1), transfer the name (with Schedule paper and number) of every child found in any institution designed for the care of poor or homeless children, or in any poor-house or other asylum for the destitute, from Schedule No. 1 to this Special Schedule, and proceed to ask the additional questions indicated in the headings of the several columns. Special attention is called to the questions respecting the child's antecedents, which are designed to bring out the proportion of children in institutions who belong to the respectable and to the vicious classes severally.

The lower part of the second part gave the following rules:
**NOTE A** – Children in institutions may not be residents of the county or State in which the institution is situated, and in that case their residence when at home should be stated, in order that they may be accredited to the State to which

he properly belongs, and that the county in which the institution is situated may not be charged with more that its due proportion of dependent children.

**NOTE B** – In making entries in columns 18, 19, and 20, an affirmative mark only will be used, thus /.

The questions asked:

1. Number taken from Schedule 1. Number of page.
2. Number taken from Schedule 1. Number of line.
3. Name.
4. Residence when at home. (See Note A.) City or Town.
5. Residence when at home. (See Note A.) County (if in same State), or State (if in some other State).
6. Is this child's father deceased?
7. Is this child's mother deceased?
8. Has this child been abandoned by his (or her) parents?
9. Has this child's parent's surrendered the control over him (or her) to the institution?
10. Was this child born in the institution?
11. If not so born, state year when admitted.
12. Is the child Illegitimate?
13. Is this child separated from his or her (living) mother?
14. Antecedents. Has he (or she) ever been arrested? If yes, for what alleged offense?
15. Antecedents. Has he (or she) ever been convicted or sentenced?
16. Antecedents. Has the origin of this child been respectable?
17. Antecedents. Has he (or she) been rescued from criminal surroundings?
18. See Note B. Is this child blind?
19. See Note B. Is he (or she) a deaf-mute?

20. See Note B. Is he (or she) an idiot?

The HOMELESS CHILDREN Schedule follows in two parts:

# 1880 Supplemental Schedule 6, for the Defective, Dependent, and Delinquent Classes

Inhabitants in _____, in the County of _____, State of _____

Enumerated by me June, 1880.

Supervisor's Dist No. _____

Enumeration Dist No. _____

## HOMELESS CHILDREN.

The object of this Supplemental Schedule is to furnish material not only for a complete enumeration of children in institutions, but for an account of their condition. It is important that every inquiry respecting each case be answered as fully as possible. Enumerators will, therefore, *after making the proper entries upon the Population Schedule (No. 1)* transfer the name (with Schedule paper and number) of every child found in any institution designed for the care of poor or homeless children, or in any poor-house or other asylum for the destitute, from Schedule No. 1 to this Special Schedule, and proceed to ask the *additional questions* indicated in the headings of the several columns. Special attention is called to the questions respecting the child's antecedents, which are designed to bring out the proportion of children in institutions who belong to the respectable and to the vicious classes severally.

| Number taken from Schedule No. 1. | | Name | Residence when at home. (See Note A.) | | Is this child's father deceased? | Is this child's mother deceased? | Has this child been abandoned by his (or her) parents? | Has this child's parent's surrendered the control over him (or her) to the institution? | Was this child born in the institution? | If not so born, state year when admitted. | Is the child illegitimate? | Is this child separated from his or her (living) mother? |
|---|---|---|---|---|---|---|---|---|---|---|---|---|
| Number of page. | Number of line. | | City or Town. | County (if in same State), or State (if in some other State). | | | | | | | | |
| 1 | 2 | 3 | 4 | 5 | 6 | 7 | 8 | 9 | 10 | 11 | 12 | 13 |
| 1 | | | | | | | | | | | | |
| 2 | | | | | | | | | | | | |
| 3 | | | | | | | | | | | | |
| 4 | | | | | | | | | | | | |
| 5 | | | | | | | | | | | | |

| Antecedents. | | | | See Note B. | | |
| --- | --- | --- | --- | --- | --- | --- |
| Has he (or she) ever been arrested? If yes, for what alleged offense? | Has he (or she) ever been convicted or sentenced? | Has the origin of this child been respectable? | Has he (or she) been rescued from criminal surroundings? | Is this child blind? | Is he (or she) a deaf-mute? | Is he (or she) an idiot? |
| 14 | 15 | 16 | 17 | 18 | 19 | 20 |
| 1 | | | | | | |
| 2 | | | | | | |
| 3 | | | | | | |
| 4 | | | | | | |
| 5 | | | | | | |

NOTE A – Children in institutions may not be residents of the county or State in which the institution is situated, and in that case their residence when at home should be stated, in order that they may be accredited to the State or county to which he properly belongs, and that the county in which the institution is situated may not be charged with more than its due proportion of dependent children.

NOTE B – In making entries in columns 18, 19, and 20, an affirmative mark only will be used, thus /

50

# Chapter Nine. Supplemental Schedule 7

SCHEDULE 7 – PRISONERS (Supplemental #6)

1880 Supplement Schedule 7, for the Defective, Dependent, and Delinquent Classes – INHABITANTS IN PRISON.

The PRISONER Schedule instructions stated:
'The object of this Supplemental is to furnish material not only for a complete enumeration of the prisoners, but for an account of their condition. It is important that every inquiry respecting each case be answered as fully as possible. Enumerators will, therefore, after making the proper entries upon the Population schedule (No. 1), transfer the name (with Schedule paper and number) of every Prisoner found, from schedule No. 1 to this Special Schedule, and proceed to ask the additional questions indicated in the headings of the several columns.

In addition to the enumeration of prisoners required in this Special Schedule, enumerators will also, in all cases (even though there should not be any prisoners in confinement upon the first of June), ask the warden or keeper of every prison, station-house, or lock-up in their respective districts the questions found below, at the bottom of the page, respecting the number of prisoners in confinement during the year ending May 21, 1880, and record the answers.'

The lower part of the second part gave the following rules:
**NOTE A** – Prisoners may not be residents of the county or State in which the prison, station-house, or lock-up is situated, and in that case their residence when at home, or the place where they were arrested or tried, should be

stated, in order that they may be accredited to the state or county to which they properly belong, and that the county in which the prison, station-house, or lock-up is situated may not be charged with more that its due proportion of prisoners.

**NOTE B** – In making entries in columns 8, 9, 10, 11, 12, 13, 14, and 15, an affirmative mark only will be used, thus: /.

The questions asked:

1. Number taken from Schedule No. 1. Number of page.
2. Number taken from Schedule No. 1. Number of line.
3. Name.
4. Residence when at home. (See Note A.) City or Town.
5. Residence when at home. (See Note A.) County (if in same State), or State (if in some other State).
6. Place of imprisonment: (State penitentiary or prison, county penitentiary or jail, work-house, house of correction, city prison, station-house, lock-up, or calaboose.)
7. Is this person a United States, State, or city prisoner? (If United States, say "U.S.")
8. Why in prison (See Note B.) Is he or she awaiting trial?
9. Why in prison (See Note B.) Is he or she serving a term of imprisonment?
10. Why in prison (See Note B.) Is he or she serving out a fine?
11. Why in prison (See Note B.) Is he or she awaiting execution (death)?
12. Why in prison (See Note B.) Is he or she sentenced to some higher prison and awaiting removal?
13. Why in prison (See Note B.) Is he or she held as a witness?

14. Why in prison (See Note B.) Is he or she imprisoned for debt?

15. Why in prison (See Note B.) Is he or she imprisoned for insanity?

16. Date of incarceration. (Give day of month and the year, the latter in two figures, thus: Jan. 15, '79.)

17. Alleged offense.

18. Sentence. Amount of fine imposed.

19. Sentence. Number of days in jail or work-house.

20. Sentence. Number of years in penitentiary.

21. Is this prisoner, at hard labor? If yes, what? (Shoe shop, cigar shop, cooper shop, stone cutting, prison duties, mining, labor on farm or plantations, etc.)

22. If at hard labor, is he or she working inside or outside the prison wall?

23. Is his or her labor contracted out?


Additional Questions to be asked of the chief executive officer of each and all prisons in the United States.

QUESTION 1 – What is the total number of persons who have been imprisoned in the _____ (a), in the county of _____, State of _____, during the year ending May 31, 1880? Answer: _____ .

QUESTION 2 – Of this total number, how many have been imprisoned in the said prison to serve out sentences imposed for crimes and misdemeanors? Total _____. Native white males, _____ ; native colored males, _____ ; native white females, _____; native colored females, _____ ; foreign males, _____ ; foreign females, _____ .

QUESTION 3 – How many have been held upon other grounds, as debtors, witnesses, insane, or pending trial, without having been convicted of any offense? Total _____ .

Native white males, _____ ; native colored males, _____ ;
native white females, _____ ; native colored females,
_____ ; foreign males, _____ ; foreign females, _____ .

QUESTION 4 − What is the total number of day's
imprisonment during the year ending May 31, 1880, of all
persons who have been confined in this prison? _____.
(This number is to be found by adding the number of days'
imprisonment of each prisoner and stating the sum.)

QUESTION 5 − Is payment made for maintenance of
prisoners by a per diem allowance to the sheriff, jailor, or
keeper? _____ ; and if yes, h ow many cents a day? _____;
what was the total amount of this per diem allowance
during the year ending May 31, 1880? $_____ - If no such
allowance is made, state the actual cost of maintenance of
prisoners during the year. $_____.

(a) Name of prison.


The PRISONERS Schedule follows in two parts:

# 1880 Supplemental Schedule 7, for the Defective, Dependent, and Delinquent Classes

Inhabitants in _____ , in the County of _____ , State of _____

Enumerated by me June, 1880.

Supervisor's Dist No. _____

Enumeration Dist No. _____

## INHABITANTS IN PRISON.

The object of this Supplemental Schedule is to furnish material not only for a complete enumeration of the prisoners, but for an account of their condition. It is important that every inquiry respecting each case be answered as fully as possible. Enumerators will, therefore, *after making the proper entries upon the Population Schedule (No. 1),* transfer the name (with Schedule paper and number) of every id of found, from Schedule No. 1 to this Special Schedule, and proceed to ask the *additional questions* indicated in the headings of the several columns

In addition to the enumeration of prisoners required in this Special Schedule, enumerators will also, in all cases (even though there should not be any prisoners in confinement upon the first of June), ask the warden or keeper of every prison, station-house, or lock-up in their respective districts the questions found below, at the bottom of the page, respecting the number of prisoners in confinement *during the year ending May 31, 1880,* and record the answers.

| Number taken from Schedule No 1 | | Name | Residence when at home. (See Note A.) | | Place of imprisonment (State penitentiary or prison, county penitentiary or jail, work-house, house of correction, city prison, station-house, lock-up, or calaboose) | Is this person a United States, State, or city prisoner? (if United States, say "U. S.") |
| Number of page | Number of line | | City or Town. | County (if in same State), or State (if in some other State) | | |
| 1 | 2 | 3 | 4 | 5 | 6 | 7 |
| 1 | | | | | | |
| 2 | | | | | | |
| 3 | | | | | | |

| | Why in prison (See Note B) | | | | | | | | Date of incarceration. (Give day of month and the year, the latter in two figures, thus Jan. 15, '79.) | Alleged offense | Sentence | | | Is this prisoner, at hard labor? If yes, what? (Shoe shop, cigar shop, cooper shop, stone cutting, prison duties, mining, labor on farm or plantations, etc.) | If at hard labor, is he or she working inside or outside the prison walls? | Is his or her labor contracted out? |
|---|---|---|---|---|---|---|---|---|---|---|---|---|---|---|---|---|
| | Is he or she awaiting trial? | Is he or she serving a term of imprisonment? | Is he or she serving out a fine? | Is he or she awaiting execution (death)? | Is he or she sentenced to some higher prison and awaiting removal? | Is he or she held as a witness? | Is he or she imprisoned for debt? | Is he or she imprisoned for insanity? | | | Amount of fine imposed | Number of days in jail or work-house. | Number of years in penitentiary | | | |
| | 8 | 9 | 10 | 11 | 12 | 13 | 14 | 15 | 16 | 17 | 18 | 19 | 20 | 21 | 22 | 23 |
| 1 | | | | | | | | | | | | | | | | |
| 2 | | | | | | | | | | | | | | | | |
| 3 | | | | | | | | | | | | | | | | |

NOTE A.—Prisoners may not be residents of the county or State in which the prison, station-house, or lock-up is situated, and in that case their residence when at home, or the place where they were arrested or tried, should be stated, in order that they may be accredited to the State or county to which they properly belong, and that the county in which the prison, station-house, or lock-up is situated may not be charged with more that its due proportion of prisoners.

NOTE B.—In making entries in columns 8, 9, 10, 11, 12, 13, 14, and 15, an affirmative mark only will be used, thus: 1.

## Additional Questions to be asked of the chief executive officer of each and all prisons in the United States.

Question 1 – What is the total number of persons who have been imprisoned in the _____ (a) _____, State of _____, during the year ending May 31, 1880? Answer.

Question 2 – Of this total number, how many have been imprisoned in the said prison to serve out sentences imposed for crimes and misdemeanors? Total _____ Native white males, _____ native colored males, _____ native white females, _____ native colored females, _____ foreign males, _____ foreign females, _____.

Question 3 – How many have been held upon other grounds, as debtors, witnesses, insane, or pending trial, without having been convicted of any offense? Total _____ Native white males _____, Native white m des, _____ native colored males, _____ native colored females, _____ foreign males, _____ foreign females, _____.

Question 4 – What is the total number of days' imprisonment during the year ending May 31, 1880, of all persons who have been confined in this prison? _____ (This number is to be found by adding the number of days' imprisonment of each prisoner and stating the sum.)

Question 5 – Is payment made for maintenance of prisoners by a per diem allowance to the sheriff, jailor, or keeper? _____ and if yes, how many cents a day? _____ what was the total amount of this per diem allowance during the year ending May 31, 1880? $ _____ — If no such allowance is made, state the actual cost of maintenance of prisoners during the year $ _____

(a) in the county of _____.
b) Name of prison

# Chapter Ten. Supplemental Schedule 7A

SCHEDULE 7A – PAUPER and INDIGENT (Supplemental #7)

1880 Supplement Schedule 7 [7A], for the Defective, Dependent, and Delinquent Classes – PAUPER AND INDIGENT.

Pauper and Indigent inhabitants (in institutions, poor-houses or asylums, or boarded at public expense in private houses) in ___, in the County of _____, State of _____, June 1, 1880.

The PAUPER and INDIGENT Schedule upper instructions stated:

'The object of this Supplemental Schedule is to furnish material not only for a complete enumeration of paupers, but for an account of their condition. It is important that every inquiry respecting each case be answered as fully as possible. Enumerators will, therefore, after making the proper entries upon the population schedule (No. 1), transfer the name (with schedule page and number) to this Special Schedule, and proceed to ask the additional questions indicated in the headings of the several columns.

In case any person enumerated on this Special Schedule is blind, deaf and dumb, insane, or idiotic (see columns 25 to 28 inclusive), the particulars of such case will also be carried on such other Special Schedule, as the case may be.

In addition to the enumeration of paupers required in this Schedule, enumerators will also ask the keeper of every institution designed for the maintenance of the destitute the questions found below, at the bottom of the page, respecting the number of paupers during the year ending May 31, 1880, and record the answers.'

The lower part of the second part gave the following rules:
NOTE A — Paupers may not be residents of the county or State in which the institution designed for the maintenance of the destitute is situated, and in that case their residence when at home, or the place from whence they came to such institution, should be stated, in order that they may be accredited to the State or county to which they properly belong, and that the county in which the institution is situated may not be charged with more than its due proportion of paupers.
NOTE B — In Making entries in columns 6, 7, 8, 9, 15, 17, 18, 19, 20, 25, 26, 27, and 28 inclusive, an affirmative mark only will be used, thus: "/." In columns 10, 11, 12, and 13 inclusive, say "Yes" or "No." as the case may be. Columns 21, 22, 23 and 24 should be filled by inserting the numbers which correctly answer the query: How may sons, daughters, brothers, sisters, respectively, has this person in this institution? — If none, use the zero (0).

The questions asked:
1. Number taken from Schedule No. 1. Number of page.
2. Number taken from Schedule No. 1. Number of line.
3. Name.
4. Residence when at home. (See Note A.) City or Town.
5. Residence when at home. (See Note A.) County (if in same State), or State (if in some other State).
6. How Supported? (See Note B.) At cost of city or town? /.
7. How Supported? (See Note B.) At cost of county? /.
8. How Supported? (See Note B.) At cost of State? /.

9. How Supported? (See Note B.) At cost of institution? /.

10. Is this person able-bodied?

11. Is he (or she) habitually intemperate?

12. Is he (or she) epileptic?

13. Has he (or she) ever been convicted of crime?

14. If disabled, state form of disability (crippled, consumption, dropsy, old age, lying-in, etc.)

15. Was this person born in this institution? /.

16. Date of admission. (Give day of month and the year, the latter in two figures, thus: "Jan. 15, '79.")

17. What other members of the family of this person are in this establishment? (See Note B.) Husband? /.

18. What other members of the family of this person are in this establishment? (See Note B.) Wife? /.

19. What other members of the family of this person are in this establishment? (See Note B.) Mother? /.

20. What other members of the family of this person are in this establishment? (See Note B.) Father? /.

21. What other members of the family of this person are in this establishment? (See Note B.) Sons – how many?

22. What other members of the family of this person are in this establishment? (See Note B.) Daughters – how many?

23. What other members of the family of this person are in this establishment? (See Note B.) Brothers – how many?

24. What other members of the family of this person are in this establishment? (See Note B.) Sisters – How many?

25. (See Note B) Is this person also blind? /.

26. (See Note B) Is he or she deaf and dumb? /.

27. (See Note B) Is he or she insane? /.

28. (See Note B) Is he or she idiotic? /.

ADDITIONAL QUESTIONS to be asked of the chief executive officer of each and all pauper establishments (including homes and asylums for the aged, for the destitute, and for the friendless) in the United States.

QUESTION 1. What is the total number of persons who have been inmates of this institution at an time for longer or shorter period, during the year ending May 31, 1880? – Answer: Total _____; native white males, _____; native colored males, _____; native white females, _____; native colored females, _____; foreign males, _____; foreign females, _____.

QUESTION 2. What is the total number of days' board furnished to inmates during the year ending May 31, 1880? – Answer: _____. This number is to be found by taking the sum of the number of days' board furnished to each inmate. By days' broad is meant the number of days during which each person was retained as an inmate.)

QUESTION 3. If paupers in this establishment are supported at the expense of the town, county, or State, is payment make for their maintenance by a weekly or monthly allowance to the keeper? – Answer: _____; and if yes, how much is the said allowance? – Answer: $_____ per _____. What was the total amount of such allowance during the year ending May 31, 1880? – Answer: $_____.

QUESTION 4. If no such allowance is made, what was the actual cost of maintenance of pauper or destitute inmate of the institution during the year ending May 31, 1880? Answer: $_____.

The enumerator in each district will also ascertain, if possible, and state the name (_____), official title or position (_____), and post-office address (_____) of the supervisor, superintendent, overseer, poor-master, or other town, city, or county officer who is charged with the relief of the poor at their own homes or elsewhere outside of institutions, in order that inquiries may be hereafter addressed to them (by mail) respecting the amount and cost of out-door relief.

The PAUPER and INDIGENT Schedule follows in two parts:

## 1880 Supplemental Schedule 7, for the Defective, Dependent, and Delinquent Classes

Pauper and Indigent inhabitants (in institutions, poor-houses or asylums, or boarded at public expense in private houses) in _____, in the County of _____, State of _____, _____ June 1, 1880.　Supervisor's Dist No. _____　Enumeration Dist No. _____

## PAUPER AND INDIGENT.

The object of this Supplemental Schedule is to furnish material and only for a complete enumeration of paupers, but for an account of their condition. It is important that every inquiry respecting each case be answered as fully as possible. Enumerators will, therefore, *after making the proper entries upon the Population Schedule (No. 1)* transfer the name (with schedule page and number) to this Special Schedule, and proceed to ask the *additional questions* indicated in the headings of the several columns.

In case any person enumerated on this Special Schedule is blind, deaf and dumb, insane, or idiotic (see columns 25 to 28 inclusive), the particulars of such case will also be carried on such other Special Schedule, as the case may be.

In addition to the enumeration of paupers required in this Schedule, enumerators will also ask the keeper of every institution designed for the maintenance of the destitute the questions found below, at the bottom of the page, respecting the number of paupers during the year ending May 31, 1880, and record the answers.

| Number taken from Schedule No 1 | | Name | Residence when at home. (See Note A.) | | How Supported? (See Note B.) | | | | Is this person able-bodied? | Is he (or she) habitually intemperate? | Is he (or she) epileptic? | Has he (or she) ever been convicted of crime? |
| Number of page | Number of line | | City or Town. | County (if in same State), or State (if in some other State). | At cost of city or town? | At cost of county? | At cost of State? | At cost of institution? | | | | |
| 1 | 2 | 3 | 4 | 5 | 6 | 7 | 8 | 9 | 10 | 11 | 12 | 13 |
| 1 | | | | | | | | | | | | |
| 2 | | | | | | | | | | | | |
| 3 | | | | | | | | | | | | |
| 4 | | | | | | | | | | | | |
| 5 | | | | | | | | | | | | |

| If disabled, state form of disability (crippled, consumption, dropsy, old age, lying-in, etc.) | Was this person born in this institution? / (See Note B) | Date of admission (Give day of month and the latter in two figures, thus "Jan. 15, '79.") | What other members of the family of this person are in this establishment? (See Note B.) | | | | | | | | (See Note B) | | | |
| 14 | 15 | 16 | Husband? / | Wife? / | Mother? / | Father? / | Sons – how many? | Daughters – how many? | Brothers – how many? | Sisters – how many? | Is this person also blind? / | Is he or she deaf and dumb? / | Is he or she insane? / | Is he or she idiotic? / |
| | | | 17 | 18 | 19 | 20 | 21 | 22 | 23 | 24 | 25 | 26 | 27 | 28 |
| 1 | | | | | | | | | | | | | | |
| 2 | | | | | | | | | | | | | | |
| 3 | | | | | | | | | | | | | | |
| 4 | | | | | | | | | | | | | | |
| 5 | | | | | | | | | | | | | | |

**NOTE A** – Paupers may not be residents of the county or State in which the institution designed for the maintenance of the destitute is situated, and in that case their residence when at home, or the place from whence they came to such institution, should be stated, in order that they may be accredited to the State or county to which they properly belong, and that the county in which the institution is situated may not be charged with more than its due proportion of paupers.

**NOTE B** – In Making entries in columns 6, 7, 8, 9, 15, 17, 18, 19, 20, 25, 26, 27, and 28 inclusive, an affirmative mark only will be used, thus "/" In columns 10, 11, 12, and 13 inclusive, say "Yes" or "No," as the case may be. Columns 21, 22, 23, and 24 should be filled by inserting the numbers which correctly answer the query. How many sons, daughters, brothers, sisters, respectively, has this person in this institution? If none, use the zero (0).

ADDITIONAL QUESTIONS to be asked of the chief executive officer of each and all pauper establishments (including homes and asylums for the aged, for the destitute, and for the friendless) in the United States.

Question 1  What is the total number of persons who have been inmates of this institution at any time for a longer or shorter period, during the year ending May 31, 1880? –Answer  Total _____ native white males, _____ native white males, _____ native coloured males, _____ females, _____ native coloured females, _____ foreign males, _____ foreign females.

Question 2  What is the total number of days' board furnished to inmates during the year ending May 31, 1880? –Answer _____  (This number is to be found by taking the sum of the number of days' board furnished to each inmate. By days' board is meant the number of days during which each person was supported at the expense of the town, county, or State, is payment made for their maintenance by a weekly or monthly allowance to the keeper? –Answer _____ and if yes, how much is the aid allowance? –Answer $ _____

Question 3  If paupers in this establishment are supported at the expense of the town, county, as State, is payment made for their maintenance by a weekly or monthly allowance to the keeper? –Answer _____ and if yes, how much is the aid allowance? –Answer $ _____ per _____  What was the total amount of such allowance during the year ending May 31, 1880? –Answer $ _____

Question 4  If no such allowance is made, whatever the actual cost of maintenance of pauper or destitute inmates of the institution during the year ending May 31, 1880? –Answer $ _____

The enumerator in each district will also ascertain, if possible, and state the name ( _____ ) official title or position ( _____ ) of the supervisor, superintendent, overseer, poor-masks, or other town, city, or county officer who is charged with the relief of the poor at their own home or elsewhere outside of institution, in order that inquiries may be hereafter addressed to them (by mail) respecting the amount and cost of out-door relief.

# Chapter Eleven. Schedule 2

Agricultural Schedule, Schedule 2.

Census office Form 7-306.

The Agricultural Schedule is known as Schedule 2. It is not called a Supplement.

The Agricultural Schedule asks 100 questions of a person which gives further insight into a person and the life of a family.

The Agricultural Census Heading:
Schedule 2 – Productions of Agricultural in _____ in the County of _____, State of _____. Enumerated by me, on the _____ day of June, 1880 _____ enumerator.

Questions asked: 100.

Note: Bush means bushel; Dolls means dollars; Doz means dozen; Galls means gallons; No means number.

1. Name of the person who Conducts the Farm. Name.
2. Tenure. Owner.
3. Rents for fixed money rental.
4. Rents for shares of products.
5. Acres of Land. Improved. Tilled.
6. Acres of Land. Improved. Permanent Meadow, Pastures, Orchards, and Vineyards.
7. Acres of Land. Unimproved. Woodland.
8. Acres of Land. Unimproved. Other unimproved.

9. Farm Value. Of Farm. Dolls.

10. Farm Value. Of Farming Implements and Machinery. Dolls.

11. Farm Value. Of Live Stock. Dolls.

12. Fences. Cost of building and repairing in 1879. Dolls.

13. Cost of Fertilizers purchased in 1879. Dolls.

14. Labor. Farm labor hiring 1879 including. Dolls.

15. Labor. Weeks hired labor in 1879 upon farm.

16. Estimated value of all farm productions for 1879. Dolls.

17. Grass Lands. Acreage 1879. Mown.

18. Grass Lands. Acreage 1879. Not Mown.

19. Grass Lands. Products harvested in 1879. Hay. Tons.

20. Grass Lands. Products harvested in 1879. Clover Seed. Bush.

21. Grass Lands. Products harvested in 1879. Grass Seed. Bush.

22. Horses of all ages on hand June 1, 1880. No.

23. Mules and Asses, all ages on hand June 1, 1880. No.

24. Meat Cattle and their Products. On Hand June 1, 1880. Working Oxen. No.

25. Meat Cattle and their Products. On Hand June 1, 1880. Milch Cows. No. [Milk Cows.]

26. Meat Cattle and their Products. On Hand June 1, 1880. Other. No.

27. Meat Cattle and their Products. Movement, 1879. Calves dropped. No.

28. Meat Cattle and their Products. Movement, 1879. Cattle of all ages. Purchased. No.

29. Meat Cattle and their Products. Movement, 1879. Cattle of all ages. Sold living. No.

30. Meat Cattle and their Products. Movement, 1879. Cattle of all ages. Slaughtered. No.

31. Meat Cattle and their Products. Movement, 1879. Cattle of all ages. Died, strayed or stolen and not recovered. No.

32. Meat Cattle and their Products. Milk sold or sent to butter or cheese factories in 1879. Gallons.

33. Meat Cattle and their Products. Butter made on farm in 1879. Lbs.

34. Meat Cattle and their Products. Cheese made on farm in 1879. Lbs.

35. Meat Cattle and their Products. On hand June 1, 1880. No.

36. Sheep. Movement 1879. Lambs dropped. No.

37. Sheep Movement 1879. Sheep and Lambs. Purchased. No.

38. Sheep Movement 1879. Sheep and Lambs. Sold living. No.

39. Sheep Movement 1879. Sheep and Lambs. Slaughtered. No.

40. Sheep Movement 1879. Sheep and Lambs. Killed by dogs. No.

41. Sheep Movement 1879. Sheep and Lambs. Died of Disease. No.

42. Sheep Movement 1879. Sheep and Lambs. Died of stress of weather. No.

43. Clip, Spring 1880, Shorn and to Shorn. Fleece. No.

44. Clip, Spring 1880, Shorn and to Shorn. Weight. Lbs.

45. Swine. On Hand June 1, 1880. No.

46. Poultry on Hand June 1, 1880 excluding Spring hatching. Barnyard. No.

47. Poultry on Hand June 1, 1880 excluding Spring hatching. Other. No.

48. Egg production during 1879. Doz.

49. Cereals. 1879. Area. Acres.

50. Cereals. Barley 1879. Crop. Bush.

51. Cereals. Buckwheat 1879. Area. Acres.

52. Cereals. Buckwheat 1879. Crop. Bush.

53. Cereals. Indian Corn 1879. Area. Acres.

54. Cereals. Indian Corn 1879. Crop. Bush.

55. Cereals. Oats 1879. Area. Acres.

56. Cereals. Oats 1879. Crop. Bush.

57. Cereals. Rye 1879. Area. Acres.

58. Cereals. Rye 1879. Crop. Bush.

59. Cereals. Wheat 1879. Area. Acres.

60. Cereals. Wheat 1879. Crop. Bush.

61. Pulse. Canadian Peas 1879. Bush.

62. Pulse. Beans 1879. Bush.

63. Fiber. Flax 1879. Area in Crop. Acres.

64. Fiber. Flax 1879. Sued. Bush.

65. Fiber. Flax 1879. Straw. Tons.

66. Fiber. Flax 1879. Fiber. Lbs.

67. Fiber. Hemp. Acres.

68. Fiber. Hemp. Ton.

69. Sugar. Sorghum 1879. Area in Crop. Acres.

70. Sugar. Sorghum 1879. Sugar. Lbs.

71. Sugar. Sorghum 1879. Molasses. Galls.

72. Sugar. Maple 1879. Sugar. Lbs.

73. Sugar. Maple 1879. Molasses. Galls.

74. Broom Corn 1879. Ace.

75. Broom Corn 1879. Lbs.

76. Hops 1879. Area. Acres.

77. Hops 1879. Crop. Lbs.

78. Potatoes (Irish) 1879. Area. Acres.

79. Potatoes (Irish) 1879. Crop. Bush.

80. Potatoes (Sweet) 1879. Area. Acres.

81. Potatoes (Sweet) 1879. Crop. Bush.

82, Tobacco 1879. Area. Acres.

83. Tobacco 1879. Crop. Lbs.

84. Orchards 1879. Apples. Acres. No.

85. Orchards 1879. Apples. Bearing Trees. No.

86. Orchards 1879. Apples. Bushels 1879. No.

87. Orchards 1879. Peaches. Acres. No.

88. Orchards 1879. Peaches. Bearing Trees. No.

89. Orchards 1879. Peaches. Bushels 1879. No.

90. Total value of Orchard Products of all kinds sold or consumed. Dolls.

91. Nurseries. Acres. No.

92. Nurseries. Value of Products sold. Dolls.

93. Vineyards. Acres. No.

94. Vineyards. Grapes sold 1879. Lbs.

95. Vineyards. Wine Made 1879. Gallons.

96. Market Gardens. Value of Products sold 1879. Dolls.

97. Bees 1879. Honey. Lbs.

98. Bees 1879. Wax. Lbs.

99. Forest Products. Amount of Wood cut in 1879. Cords.

100. Forest Products. Value of all forest products sold or consumed in 1879. Dolls.

Following shows the Agricultural Schedule in four parts.

# 1880 Agricultural Census Schedule

Schedule 2 – Productions of Agriculture in _____ in the County of _____, State of _____

Enumerated by me, on the _____ day of June, 1880 _____ enumerator

| Name of the Person who Conducts the Farm | Tenure | | | | Acres of Land | | | | | | Farm Value | | | Fences | Cost of Fertilizers purchased in 1879 | Labor | | Estimated value of all farm productions for 1879 | Grass Lands | | | | | | Horses of all ages on hand June 1, 1880 | Mules and Asses, all ages on hand June 1, 1880 |
| | | | | | Improved | | Unimproved | | | | | | | | | | | | Acreage 1879 | | Products harvested in 1879 | | | | |
| Name | Owner | Rents for fixed money rental | Rents for shares of products | Tilled | Permanent Meadows, Pastures, Orchards, and Vineyards | Woodland and forest | Other unimproved | | Of Farm | Of Farming Implements and Machinery | Of Live Stock | Cost of building and repairing in 1879 | | farm labor 1879 including hiring | Weeks hired labor in 1879 upon farm. | | Mown | Not Mown | Hay | Clover Seed | Grass Seed | | |
| | | | | No | No | No | No | | Dolls | Dolls | Dolls | Dolls | Dolls | Dolls | No | Dolls | Acres | Acres | Tons | Bush | Bush | No | No |
| | 2 | 3 | 4 | 5 | 6 | 7 | 8 | | 9 | 10 | 11 | 12 | 13 | 14 | 15 | 16 | 17 | 18 | 19 | 20 | 21 | 22 | 23 |
| 1 | | | | | | | | | | | | | | | | | | | | | | | |
| 1 | | | | | | | | | | | | | | | | | | | | | | | |
| 2 | | | | | | | | | | | | | | | | | | | | | | | |
| 3 | | | | | | | | | | | | | | | | | | | | | | | |

| | Neat Cattle and their Products | | | | | | | | | | | | Sheep | | | | | | | | | | Swine | Poultry On Hand June 1, 1880 excluding Spring hatching | | |
| | On Hand June 1, 1880 | | | Movement, 1879 — Cattle of all ages | | | | | Milk Sold or sent to butter or cheese factories in 1879 | Butter made on farm in 1879 | Cheese made on farm in 1879 | On hand June 1, 1880 | Movement, 1879 — Sheep and Lambs | | | | | | | Clip, Spring 1880, Shorn and to Shorn | | On Hand June 1, 1880 | | | Egg production during 1879 |
| | Working Oxen | Milch Cows | Other | Calves Dropped | Purchased | Sold living | Slaughtered | Died, strayed or stolen and not recovered | | | | | Lambs dropped | Purchased | Sold living | Slaughtered | Killed by dogs | Died of Disease | Died of stress of weather | Fleece | Weight | | Barnyard | Other | |
| | No | No | No | No | No | No | No | No | Gallons | Lbs | Lbs | No | No | No | No | No | No | No | No | No | Lbs | No | No | No | Doz |
| | 24 | 25 | 26 | 27 | 28 | 29 | 30 | 31 | 32 | 33 | 34 | 35 | 36 | 37 | 38 | 39 | 40 | 41 | 42 | 43 | 44 | 45 | 46 | 47 | 48 |
| 1 | | | | | | | | | | | | | | | | | | | | | | | | | |
| 2 | | | | | | | | | | | | | | | | | | | | | | | | | |
| 3 | | | | | | | | | | | | | | | | | | | | | | | | | |

**Table 1**

| | Barley 1879 | | Buckwheat 1879 | | Cereals — Indian Corn 1879 | | Oats 1879 | | Rye 1879 | | Wheat 1879 | | Pulse — Canadian Peas 1879 | Beans 1879 | Flax 1879 — Fiber | | | | Hemp | | Sorghum 1879 | | | Sugar — Maple 1879 | | Broom Corn 1879 | |
|---|---|---|---|---|---|---|---|---|---|---|---|---|---|---|---|---|---|---|---|---|---|---|---|---|---|---|---|---|
| | Area | Crop | Area | Crop | Area | Crop | Area | Crop | Area | Crop | Area | Crop | | | Area in Crop | Seed | Straw | Fiber | | | Area in Crop | Sugar | Molasses | Sugar | Molasses | | |
| | Acres | Bush | Acres | Bush | Acres | Bush | Acres | Bush | Acres | Bush | Acres | Bush | Bush | Bush | Acres | Bush | Tons | Lbs | Acs | Ton | Acres | Lbs | Galls | Lbs | Galls | Acs | Lbs |
| | 49 | 50 | 51 | 52 | 53 | 54 | 55 | 56 | 57 | 58 | 59 | 60 | 61 | 62 | 63 | 64 | 65 | 66 | 67 | 68 | 69 | 70 | 71 | 72 | 73 | 74 | 75 |
| 1 | | | | | | | | | | | | | | | | | | | | | | | | | | | |
| 2 | | | | | | | | | | | | | | | | | | | | | | | | | | | |
| 3 | | | | | | | | | | | | | | | | | | | | | | | | | | | |

**Table 2**

| | Hops 1879 | | Potatoes (Irish) 1879 | | Potatoes (Sweet) 1879 | | Tobacco 1879 | | Orchards 1879 — Apples | | | Peaches | | | Total Value of Orchard Products of all kinds sold or consumed | Nurseries | | Vineyards | | | Market Gardens | Bees 1879 | | Forest Products | |
|---|---|---|---|---|---|---|---|---|---|---|---|---|---|---|---|---|---|---|---|---|---|---|---|---|---|
| | Area | Crop | Area | Crop | Area | Crop | Area | Crop | Acres | Bearing Trees | Bushels 1879 | Acres | Bearing Trees | Bushels 1879 | | Acres | Value of Product sold | Acres | Grapes sold 1879 | Wine Made 1879 | Value of Produce sold 1879 | Honey | Wax | Amount of Wood cut in 1879 | Value of all forest product sold or consumed in 1879 |
| | Acres | Lbs | Acres | Bush | Acres | Bush | Acres | Lbs | No | No | No | No | No | No | Dolls | No | Dolls | No | Lbs | Gallons | Dolls | Lbs | Lbs | Cords | Dolls |
| | 76 | 77 | 78 | 79 | 80 | 81 | 82 | 83 | 84 | 85 | 86 | 87 | 88 | 89 | 90 | 91 | 92 | 93 | 94 | 95 | 96 | 97 | 98 | 99 | 100 |
| 1 | | | | | | | | | | | | | | | | | | | | | | | | | |
| 2 | | | | | | | | | | | | | | | | | | | | | | | | | |
| 3 | | | | | | | | | | | | | | | | | | | | | | | | | |

# Chapter Twelve. Schedule 3

Industrial and Manufacturers Census Schedule, Schedule 3. Census office Form 7-261.

The top of the Industrial and Manufacturers Schedule says: Manufactures. – Products of Industry in _____, in the County of _____, State of _____ during the twelve months beginning June 1, 1879, and ending May 31, 1880, as enumerated by me, _____ ass't Marshal.

Questions asked: 29.

1. Name of Corporation, Company, or Individual producing to the value of $500 annually.

2. Name of Business, Manufacture, or Product.

3. Capital (real or personal) invested in the business.

4. Greatest number of hands employed at any time during the year.

5. Average number of hands employed. Males above 16 years.

6. Average number of hands employed. Females above 15 years.

7. Average number of hands employed. Children and youth.

8. Wages and Hours of Labor. May to November.

9. Wages and Hours of Labor. November to May.

10. Wages and Hours of Labor. Average day's wages for skilled mechanic.

11. Wages and Hours of Labor. Average day's wages for ordinary laborer.

12. Wages and Hours of Labor. Total amount paid in wages during the year.

13. Months in Operation. On Full time.

14. Months in Operation. On 3/4 time only.

15. Months in Operation. On Full time.

16. Months in Operation. On 1/2 time only.

17. Months in Operation. Idle.

18. Value of Material (including Mill Supplies and Fuel).

19. Value of Product (including jobbing and Repairing).

20. Power Used in Manufacturing. If Water Power is Used. On what River or Stream?

21. Power Used in Manufacturing. If Water Power is Used. Wheels. Height of Fall, in feet.

22. Power Used in Manufacturing. If Water Power is Used. Wheels. Number.

23. Power Used in Manufacturing. If Water Power is Used. Wheels. Kind.

24. Power Used in Manufacturing. If Water Power is Used. Wheels. Breadth, in feet.

25. Power Used in Manufacturing. If Water Power is Used. Wheels. Revolutions per minute.

26. Power Used in Manufacturing. If Water Power is Used. Wheels. Horsepower.

27. Power Used in Manufacture. If Steam Power is Used. Number of boilers.

28. Power Used in Manufacture. If Steam Power is Used. Number of engines.

29. Power Used in Manufacture. If Steam Power is Used. Horse-power.

Following shows the Industrial and Manufacturers Schedule.

# 1880 Industrial and Manufacturers Census Schedules

Schedule 3. – Manufactures. – Products of Industry in _____, in the County of _____, State of _____ ass't Marshal during the twelve months beginning June 1, 1879, and ending May 31, 1880, as enumerated by me, _____

| Name of Corporation, Company, or Individual producing to the value of $500 annually | Name of Business, Manufacture, or Product | Capital (real or personal) invested in the business | Greatest number of hands employed at any time during the year | Average number of hands employed | | | | Wages and Hours of Labor | | | | Months in Operation | | | | | Value of Material (including Mill Supplies and Fuel) | Value of Product (including Jobbing and Repairing) | Power Used in Manufacture | | | | | | | | | | |
|---|---|---|---|---|---|---|---|---|---|---|---|---|---|---|---|---|---|---|---|---|---|---|---|---|---|---|---|---|
| | | | | Male above 16 years | Females above 15 years | Children and youth | May to November | November to May | Average day's wages for skilled mechanic | Average day's wages for ordinary laborer | Total amount paid in wages during the year | On Full time | On ¾ time only | On ⅔ time only | On ½ time only | Idle | | | If Water Power is Used | | | | | | | If Steam Power is Used | | |
| | | | | | | | | | | | | | | | | | | | Of What River or Creek Height of Fall, in feet. Steam | Number | Kind | Wheels Breadth, in feet | in feet | Revolutions per minute | Horse-power | Number of boilers | Number of engines | Horse-power |
| 1 | 2 | 3 | 4 | 5 | 6 | 7 | 8 | 9 | 10 | 11 | 12 | 13 | 14 | 15 | 16 | 17 | 18 | 19 | 20 | 22 | 23 | 24 | 25 | 26 | 27 | 28 | 29 | |

# Chapter Thirteen. Mortality Schedule

Mortality Schedule 1880 – Federal
Census office Form 7-222.

The top of the 1880 Federal Mortality Schedule stated the State, County, and Town/Township. The bottom has an area for Remarks.

Questions asked: 17.

1. Family number as given in column 2 – Schedule 1.
2. Name of the person deceased.
3. Personal Description. Age at last birthday.
4. Personal Description. Sex.
5. Personal Description. Color – (White, Black, Mulatto, Chinese, Indian).
6. Deceased status. Single.
7. Deceased status. Married.
8. Deceased status. Widowed / Divorced.
9. Nativity. The deceased place of birth, naming the State or Territory – or the Country, if of foreign birth.
10. Nativity. Where was the father born?
11. Nativity. Where was the mother born?
12. Profession, Occupation, or Trade.
13. The month in which the person died.
14. Disease or cause of death.
15. How long a resident of the county?
16. If the disease wasn't contracted at place of death, then where?
17. Name of attending Physician.

Following is the 1880 Mortality Schedule.

# 1880 FEDERAL MORTALITY SCHEDULE

State-    County-    Town/Township-

| Family number as given in column 2 – schedule 1 | Name of the person deceased | Personal Description | | | Deceased status | | | Nativity | | | Profession, Occupation, or Trade | The month in which the person died | Disease or cause of death | How long a resident of the county? | If the disease wasn't contracted at place of death, then where? | Name of attending Physician |
|---|---|---|---|---|---|---|---|---|---|---|---|---|---|---|---|---|
| | | Age at last birthday | Sex | Color - (White, Black, Mulatto, Chinese, Indian) | Single | Married | Widowed / Divorced | The deceased place of birth, naming the State or Territory, or the Country, if of foreign birth | Where was the father born? | Where was the mother born? | | | | | | |
| 1 | 2 | 3 | 4 | 5 | 6 | 7 | 8 | 9 | 10 | 11 | 12 | 13 | 14 | 15 | 16 | 17 |
| | | | | | | | | | | | | | | | | |
| | | | | | | | | | | | | | | | | |
| | | | | | | | | | | | | | | | | |
| | | | | | | | | | | | | | | | | |
| | | | | | | | | | | | | | | | | |
| | | | | | | | | | | | | | | | | |
| | | | | | | | | | | | | | | | | |
| | | | | | | | | | | | | | | | | |
| | | | | | | | | | | | | | | | | |
| | | | | | | | | | | | | | | | | |
| | | | | | | | | | | | | | | | | |
| | | | | | | | | | | | | | | | | |
| | | | | | | | | | | | | | | | | |
| | | | | | | | | | | | | | | | | |

Remarks:

# Chapter Fourteen. Finding Originals

To find all of the forms for your family member, the ones you will not find on line, you will be forced to do inquiries to ask if they have the various forms or film with the originals on the film. Don't be surprised if they do not know that there were more forms beyond Schedule 1, the main form.

Start by calling your local library and inquire with the head librarian, or if your library has a genealogy department, the head librarian in that department.

Your second call, if needed, should be to a local genealogy society if the area has one. They may be able to at least tell you where to find the schedules you want copies of.

Further inquiries should be to local universities. Some have a genealogy area or area for local history.

If you have still hit a dead end, contact your State Archives even though the census is federal.

You may want to try the Census Bureau but you will most likely be told to contact the United States National Archives. The census bureau is concerned with current and upcoming new information, not the past.

The National Archives states: "The 1880 census is indexed only for families with children age 10 years or younger. If your ancestor resided in a household that did not include a child age 10 or less, you will have to search the census of the community in which he/she lived line by line." Keep in mind that most of what you find concerning where to look refers only to the Main Schedule, Schedule 1 and those are available for most areas on some free and pay sites. Should you need to contact the National Archives, start with a free phone call: 1-866-272-6272. Remember that you want the Supplements plus Schedules 2, 3 and Mortality if your situation warrants. Information on Schedule 1 should lead you. Again, in total, there are ELEVEN different 1880 census forms.

With all of your calls, have a pencil and paper ready in case they refer you to another phone number or office.

Have patience and enjoy your hunt!

## A note from the author:

Thank you for purchasing this book.

Your positive feedback is appreciated at your place of purchase.

Further books by D. M. Kalten can be found at
http://BooksByKalten.blogspot.com/

www.ingramcontent.com/pod-product-compliance
Lightning Source LLC
Chambersburg PA
CBHW071221280526
45787CB00002B/753